IMPERFECTLY PERFECT

by
Matt Schur

First paperback edition 2023

Book and cover design by pixelstudio

ISBN 979-8-218-14279-7 (paperback)
ISBN 979-8-218-14280-3 (ebook)

For my mom, Sharon,
who has joined the saints triumphant in heaven
and who at this very moment is probably telling Jesus that she's cold,
so he needs to put on a sweater.

Ring the bells that still can ring.
Forget your perfect offering.
There is a crack, a crack in everything.
That's how the light gets in.

—Leonard Cohen, *Anthem*

TABLE OF CONTENTS

MUSINGS & STORIES

NOVEMBER

Days grow shorter
shadows grow longer
and clear cold silent nights
sometimes seem unholy.

Done disrobing
their kaleidoscope foliage fallen
at their feet
bare branches expose
starkly thin naked limbs.

The Schrödinger month between autumn and winter
a purgatory place in time
reminds our temporal bodies of the eternal truth
that as it has been, so it shall be.

Is anything truly linear?
Scientists say
time twists in on itself
and space spins back
toward its beginning.

From the vast universe
to the minuscule subatom
the cyclical passion play
embedded in the DNA of the universe
brings with it promise
hope
trust
that the annual autumnal descent toward death
eventually results in resurrection

ELI, ELI, LEMA SABACHTHANI

It was Monday.
Jesus stretched on the sunny steps
awaiting glad tidings of great joy.
Bob Marley's little birds
wailed their reassurances from a beat-up phone
and syncopated steel drum metallic melodies sang
with the guitar on the off beat.
Full-throated and smiling, Jesus sang along.
He first heard this one in college, he told me
before the legion demon voices
      the felony sex offense
      the scarlet letter marking him unclean
before hearing The Accuser's voice
denying him shelter seventy times seven times.
"You shut the door of the kingdom of heaven in people's faces,"
he mumbled to the departing rental agent.
And a freight train left Birmingham.

It was Tuesday.
Foxes have holes, birds have nests;
but other than the flattened box

behind the dumpster next to Duffy's Tavern,
dirty smelly unshaven sex offender Jesus
had nowhere to lay his head.
"Who do you say that I am?" he asked the wind.
And a freight train roared toward Memphis.

It was Wednesday.
Driven to a random flop house wilderness
serpent syringes hissed promises of escape
through glistening fangs.
"Get behind me, Satan," Jesus whispered
toward a crumpled reminder card.
And a freight train approached Springfield.

It was Thursday.
Flickering streetlights conjured dancing demons
on the pavement and across the grass
forming an unholy halo circling the head
of a solitary holy silhouette
holding a half-empty bottle of booze
and a half-empty bag of stale crackers.
"Can we meet tomorrow?" I asked.
"Do quickly what you are going to do," Jesus sighed.
"If it is possible, take this cup away from me."
And a freight train picked up speed north of Kansas City.

It was Friday.
Clouds obscured the afternoon sun
as Jesus jumped off the O Street Bridge,

his body broken for our sins
against the front of a speeding freight train
on its way to Billings.

FIREBIRD SKYSUITE

There's nothing like a glowing September sunset in Nebraska
golden cornstalks stretching
toward the infinite horizon basking
in the end-of-day lengthening rays awaiting
the coming harvest

Refractive heavenly hues
filtered through invisible teardrops and ashen discord
intone a warmly colored requiem
for the annual Promethean offerings
a thousand miles away

while the midwestern audience
watches a command performance of Stravinsky
soaked in rapt wonder
at God's creative beauty

HOLY PRESENCE

Do you see it there,
this gift you have been handed,
this fragile, breakable blood diamond
cut from the fleshy earth of the heart?
You have the power in your hand to crush it
by squeezing too tightly
or to shatter it
by letting it go completely.
Diamonds are supposed to be hard
but there's something about handing over
pain
sorrow
grief
worry
fear
that softens it in the giving
and you who now hold it?
gently caress this delicate jewel
and know that the space it once occupied
has already begun to heal

NUMBERS 14:18

The Lord is slow to anger,
and abounding in steadfast love,
forgiving iniquity and transgression,
but by no means clearing the guilty,
visiting the iniquity of the parents
upon the children
to the third and the fourth generation.

her boyfriend said he loved her
and he also beat the shit out of her
(though he couldn't say why)
until it became too much and she left him forever
    until she returned
because she loved him
(though she couldn't say why)
and he was sorry after all
and it wouldn't happen again
    until it did again
and she left again (forever)
until she returned again

one sunny summer day in her sixth month
anticipation and belly growing

he was angry drunk again
at the top of the second story stairs
and he shoved her

crumpled in the entryway
her moans and cries like wailing sirens
while blue and red emergency lights mirrored
the bluish bruises forming on her face
and the sticky red spot slowly growing between her legs.

after the stillbirth the doctors asked
did she want to see her baby (no)
did she want to know her baby's sex (no)

her childhood loomed in her memory
her own father's drunken anger
her own mother's bruises and blood
and she couldn't bear to discover if her
dead child
would someday have become

a violent father
an abusive boyfriend

a beaten mother
a pregnant girlfriend
who lies to EMTs

(she had tripped and fallen
down
the stairs, she had said
and should have been more careful she had said
but thank God for her boyfriend
who had called 911
she had said)

Is it God who passes down brokenness
to the third and fourth generations?
Is it God who punishes the innocent?
Is it God who fashions unwitting transgressors
out of the fertile soil of victimhood?

All due respect to whoever wrote
Numbers 14:11,
but no.
Hell no.

Generational trauma?
That shit is human nature.

ELEVEN DAYS AT COUNTRY ESTATES

A reverse shiva
on this side of the veil
liminal holiness, walking without steps
awaiting the fullness of time.

How long, o lord?

the answer arises in the unheard whisper
of breath leaving the body

ON THE EDGES

While I don't fancy myself a Bringer of Wisdom and Knowledge to the Masses, I am always deeply honored whenever anyone asks my opinion on some theological question, especially when that person resides on the edge of faith, as so many of my friends do. It's humbling to consider that someone who either has written off Christianity entirely or who isn't quite sure what to do with it anymore is of the opinion that I might have something of value to say.

It's interesting—I am a lifelong Christian, yet much of the time I consider these, the outliers and doubters, the fallen-away and those who have been hurt by the faith, the pagans and atheists and agnostics and Christmas-and-Easter-To-Make-the-Parental-Units-Happy, "my people."

And the older I get, the truer that becomes.

I know for certain it's not because my faith is any less than it once was. As a matter of fact, I can honestly say I believe more deeply and completely now, and that my personal faith is more embodied in my actions and the way I see the world than it has ever been at any other point in my life. I am not disillusioned with my Lutheran Christian understanding of God. In a very real sense, I'm much more traditionally orthodox than I once was, much more appreciative of the deep, ancient roots that run through patterns of worship and the words of Scripture.

The longer I live, the more deeply I explore my faith, and the more fully I flesh out my personal theology, the more I've come to recognize that faith is a messy thing. Reading and interpreting Scripture are messy things. Discerning and following God's will are messy things. But rather than being frightened by the messiness, I've found it instead to be a comfort. Because life itself is a messy thing, and any faith worth a shit is going to have to be willing to wallow in life's messiness to have any relevance whatsoever.

Even the very words of Scripture bear witness to this messy God we follow. There are contradictions. There are layers upon layers of meaning. There are different types of literature written in different times and in different places by different people. Sometimes these writings are edited and redacted and compiled, sometimes they're more interested in telling the story of God than in reporting history as a textbook, and sometimes they're the end product of hundreds of years of oral tradition finally written down. Many times, they're all these things at once.

The Bible is not just a book. It is a book of books, a beautifully messy collection. Very seldom does it claim to be a theophany, where God speaks to a person and tells that person word for word what to write. It is inspired, it is God-breathed, but it is not divinely dictated.

And that's precisely why I find the Bible believable. Because the way I see God at work in the world today is very similar.

The world is God-breathed.

The same Holy Spirit who hovered over the chaos of creation still is doing her creative work in, through, and around us, but not by way of divine dictation. No, Christ as living word works on us in far more powerful and transformative ways:

through our neighbor,
through the stranger,
through our enemy,
through the grace we extend, and the grace extended toward us,
through our questions and wrestling and doubt,
through the messiness.

So for me, there is this relentless tugging toward the edge: the uncertain edge of faith and the meeting point of belief and disbelief.

I love going there on the edge and hanging out with my friends. Maybe it's because there's no pretense. They know it's pretty damn hard to offend me, so they feel free to ask the tough questions and speak the tough truths. They often serve for me the same function as the Old Testament prophets did: speaking a voice over against the powers-that-be, and naming with clarity the errors and sins of the wider church.

They point to scripture and point to the church's activity and voice in the world, and they ask why the two don't meet up with each other in the way they should.

They point to what they see as a dusty, dry, culturally outdated book written two to four thousand years ago, and ask why they should pay any attention to it or put any stock into what it says.

They ask about contradictions and lost meanings and context in the words of Scripture, and how it all ties together.

In short, they ask the questions I also ask...and sometimes the questions I haven't asked, but should.

We don't always agree. I'm sure there have been plenty of times where the other person has walked away thinking to themselves, "the hell with that." But even in the midst of disagreement, our mutual goal is to understand the other. In the process of opening ourselves to the other, we become more fully human.

After all, we are relational beings created in the image of a relational God. So when we are open and understanding and vulnerable, we're entering more deeply into our created identity. And you know what?

Openness? It's messy.

Seeking to understand the other? Yup. Same.

Vulnerability? Does it get any more emotionally and spiritually messy than becoming vulnerable?

We are hot mess children of a messy God who lives on the edges. And I wouldn't have it any other way.

SATURDAY AT THE BAR

The shouting last Saturday began between bar band songs
and even before turning around I knew
it was going to be that guy, the one on the barstool
with the pitcher of piss-colored beer
wearing the same coat I had last seen him in three or four years back
when he stumbled off the street
whiskey shooters in his left pocket
an open 40 of Hurricane in his right pocket
years of homelessness in his back pocket
and ready for me to manage the shit
out of his case.

He was a mean drunk even then
ready to pick a fight with bloodshot eyes and wayward fists
at the hint of the possibility of the question of an insult.

Last Saturday, I didn't see what began it all or
why two men were holding him against the wall
but I remembered the time
the police had held him against the wall
to protect the poor guy he was trying to beat up
while drunk on piss colored beer
and how a few sober hours earlier that day

he had been sobbing.

Openly weeping
his silent shudders and the shaking shoulders
of an ugly man cry
telling the story he'd told me a hundred times before
about the girl who had left him.

See, when he'd miss her too much
he'd drink
and drink
and drink
until he couldn't remember her anymore
and he hated himself for it
and hated her for it
and loved her too.

Last Saturday, grief assumed the form of
a pitcher of piss-colored beer and
"I miss you" sounded like
"Get your fucking hands off me"
as he was pushed out the door
into the dark night.

MORNING MIRROR

The daily reflection staring back
Reveals an inexorable march of grey
invading my temples—
a slow invasion to be sure, but
a siege certain to ultimately result in a complete takeover.
The crows have flown the nest, leaving their footprints
along the edges of my eyes,
now adorned by bifocals.
Buttoning my shirt, I recall
the flat stomach of a young man
before it was replaced by a paunch.

Here I am on the track in the tunnel
staring at the oncoming annual physical oncoming train light
like a near-death experience.

As the good doctor stares back I'm
preparing for the flattening
by questions of my fattening
and dear God I had no idea a cholesterol number
could be that high and
where are you about to put that gloved-up hand
and I thought colonoscopies were for old people

There was a time I could stay up all night after eating half a Walmart
cheesecake
drinking half a case of Natty Lite
bright and chipper the next morning
sporting my Brandon Walsh bangs
with 90210 90s sideburns framing my ears.
I never imagined sophomore year when that girl called me cute
that eventually I'd hope for handsome
and soon I'll pray for distinguished
the distinguished gentleman with the grey
and the paunch
and the cholesterol
and the divided pillbox
and who apparently is now part of the target audience
for those old diabeetus and oatmeal Wilford Brimley ads
brought to you by AARP

Some mornings I sadly stare as through a glass darkly
at those mirrored reminders,
a little embarrassed at the reflected eye contact
remembering a body
not muscular but thin
with a forehead
not a fivehead
actually able to rise from a chair
without a single groan
but
other mornings I gird my loins

looking middle age square in the eyes,
recognizing these imperfectly perfect badges of honor
bestowed by the Creator
who saw this middle aged body
and called it good

FORTY-FIVE MILES EAST OF FORT PIERCE

Souls on board.
such a peculiar maritime accounting
as if vessels crisscrossing the ocean
under constant pursuit by Death have been overtaken
by the reaper of the deep
separating body from soul to find heaven
achieving gnostic nirvana

sailors once believed
the watery horizon was the end of the world
and they knew
in the Beginning the eternal Spirit of God
hovered over the dark face of the ancient waters
predating even light itself
as the void of night precedes the dawn

near the watery horizon
the rising sun shatters the night
revealing an overturned boat bobbing
with one soul clinging to hope and rotted wood

and in this peculiar accounting
thirty-nine other souls
hover over the face of the deep
in union with the eternal Spirit of God

GRACE

When "blessed are the peacemakers"
actually means
"blessed are the conflict avoiders"

grant me grace.

When courage means "be not afraid"
instead of "afraid but
doing the right thing anyway"

grant me grace.

when my privilege is for furthering
my own comfort
and not to further the cause
of justice

grant me grace.

when grace is for me
and my shortcomings

but not for those who need grace
from me

grant me grace.

and may that grace
empower me to empower others
bless me to be a blessing to others
live in me so that I may live for others.

GOOD WORDS

"What's the good word?" he asked
and I stumbled over a mumble
(I never know what to say).
Is there one specific good word?
Hope? Peace? Love?
Antidisestablishmentarianism is a good word
(at least it's fun to say).
Or maybe a phrase instead—
life is good?
Is it supposed to be uplifting
(Jesus loves you)
or just description
(the square root of 2,401 is 49)
though describing so much of what we see in the world
can be anything but uplifting?
Is it supposed to be a sending out
a good word benediction
an Aaronic orans hands blessing
bestowed on the hearer
like a priest consecrating a sacrament?
I never know what to say
as I stumble mumble
wishing he had just asked
"how are you?"

BIBLE THINGS &
THEOLOGY STUFF

DEATH AND RESURRECTION

Death is familiar,
an all-too intimate acquaintance
ever since Eden.

Arriving with our final breath
and all of life's finalities,
death's grip embraces us,
smothering us in its cold chest
as we struggle for air—
sometimes silently,
sometimes screaming.

but

life's grip embraces death
smothers death's power
as death struggles in its own throes
roaring as a mortally wounded lion
slowly slipping into the void
no longer ruling with suffering
        with injustice
        with fear

but being ruled by them
when resurrected life
intimately acquainted with death arises
out of a once-dead body

an empty tomb is a dead tomb

TRINITY

Isn't it all a bit queer?

unexpectedly
      and
      simultaneously
one and other
unified and differentiated
           male christ
      chromosomeless creator
      feminine spirit of wisdom
in a holy non-binary trinity
beyond doctrinal explanation

overturning divine convention
disregarding our expectation
trespassing false boundaries
creating an ever-changing universe and
        creating humanity and
          creating you
in the image of divine fluidity
           loving you

in all your unique beauty

                      orienting you

toward abundantly joyful life

Isn't it all a bit queer?

BETTY JESUS

After a particularly sucky year filled with sucky things like coup attempts, school shootings, and worldwide pandemics, 2021 was mercifully nearing its end. Tired and beaten down, Americans were looking for pretty much anything positive that we could cling to.

We found it in Betty White.

Yes, that Hollywood icon of spunk and wholesomeness was going to be celebrating her 100th birthday on January 17th, 2022. Betty's party was set to be televised, and promised to be a way for the country's collective cultural consciousness to symbolically leave 2021 in the rearview mirror and look ahead to better times.

But then, on *the very last fucking day of the year*, the Spirit of 2021 struck its cruelest blow of all.

Betty White died.

Seriously? Seriously, 2021? You couldn't even give us *this?* It felt like one last parting kick of sand in the face.

I realize this all may sound overdramatic, silly, or even stupid. Maybe it was, a little bit. After all, I'd imagine most of us would love to live a long, richly fulfilling life where we make a difference, and eventually die peacefully of natural causes. And while she was quite an amazing woman, it's not like the vast majority of us knew her on any kind of personal level.

That said, her birthday was supposed to have been a symbolic flipping of the middle finger to the year that had just ended—a event for the general public to celebrate not just her life, but the turning of the page on a year that had been a symbol of fear, death, and bad things in general.

Not long afterward, a brilliant meme by an anonymous author began making its way across social media. It read:

No.
Nope.
Betty White didn't die.
She grabbed 2021 by the throat, and whispered in its ear, "I'm taking you with me, you son of a bitch."
And then she threw them both into the fires of Mordor to save us all.
That's my fucking story and I'm sticking to it.
It is canon.

When I finished reading this meme for the first time, I literally gave a fist pump and stage whispered "YESSSSSS!!!" It took an event we were collectively mourning and reframed it as a "mama bear" moment. Sweet little Betty White wasn't just one more victim of 2021. No, she *defeated* 2021. She sacrificed herself to *kick its ass* for our sake, leaving us with a clean slate to begin 2022.

Almost sounds like a religious moment, doesn't it?

———

Buckle up, because I'm about to get a little nerdy on you here. We're gonna talk about what's called *atonement theory*.

Before we do, let's take a step back for a quick moment. "What exactly *is* an atonement theory?" you may be asking. Well, it's a way of trying to explain exactly what happened on the cross and in the empty tomb. In other words, it's meant to answer questions such as "Yeah, Jesus died and rose, but what did all of that actually do? What was the whole purpose? How are we to understand what God was up to? What mechanism was at work that made this event significant?"

There have been a bunch of different theories, different answers Christians have come up with over the centuries. Was Jesus sacrificed in humanity's place for the forgiveness of sins? Did Jesus satiate God's wrath against our sin? Or what if God make a deal with the devil to save humankind using Jesus as the ransom?

There are others, as well. They all have fancy names and were proposed at different points across history for different reasons, but none of that is really important for now.

For me, the important thing is that I don't like any of 'em.

It feels like each one focuses on just one half of the story. They attempt to speak to Jesus's death, but then they leave the resurrection as little more than an afterthought, significant only in that God doesn't remain dead.

(Okay, now stay with me here, because we're about to get to the good stuff.)

Me, I'm a big fan of the (non-Betty White) atonement theory known as *Christus Victor*, or "Christ the Victor." This understanding of the cross says that Jesus told Sin and Death (yeah, with a capital S and a capital D), "I'm taking you with me, you sons of bitches!" as he grabbed them by their throats and flung himself along with them into the fires of hell.

But the sacrifice itself wasn't enough. For humanity to realize the fullness of the victory, God couldn't just leave it at that. The resurrection was the equivalent of the climactic scene near the end of an action movie: I imagine Jesus striding confidently away from the tomb on Easter morning as it violently explodes in the background. Sin and Death do their worst, and Jesus wins anyway.

This beats the hell out of theories that focus on the reason for Jesus's death.

One theory looks like infanticide as God kills God's only son.

In another one, God seems so intent on killing *something* instead of just forgiving us for our continual screwups so instead, Jesus dies in our place to save us from God.

And in the biggest head scratcher of them all, God offers Jesus *to pay off the fucking Devil* so that humanity can be spared.

My non-Christian friends will describe one of those theories, a couple of which have become the dominant way the story's been told in America, and ask, "You've gotta be kidding me, right?"

The thing is, I totally agree with them.

I don't find those atonement theories compelling, either.

But *Christus Victor*? Sweet little Betty White Jesus ferociously clutching Sin and Death 2021 (that son of a bitch) by the throat while she throws herself into the fires of Mordor Hell?

Now *that's* what I'm talking about! Gimme some of that! The crucifixion and resurrection didn't happen because God wants it or needs it or is trying to balance out some sort of divine calculus. Instead, God is taking on the violence of Sin which leads to Death (again with the capital letters) that already exists in the world—the horrific stuff we do to each other.

Again, it feels like a movie. For the first hour and a half, we watch as the forces of Sin and Death/2021 scheme to set what seems like the perfect trap. Using captive humanity as their weapon, Sin and Death attack Betty Jesus.

And then, as the audience covers their mouths in horror, *Sin and Death/2021 actually kill Betty Jesus.*

And God lets it happen. But just before it happens, much to the twin villains' surprise, Betty Jesus grabs a hold of them by the throat.

Wait—this wasn't how it was supposed to go. Sin and Death/2021 try to free themselves, but there's nothing they can do as the struggle sends them all over the precipice. The audience can hear Sin and Death/2021 crying "NOOOOOOOO!" as they sail ever downward, straight into the fire and brimstone, Betty Jesus still gripping their throats. A couple of seconds later, a little poof of fire lets the audience know that they all have met their end, and the theater crowd goes wild at the spectacle and badassery of Betty Jesus's selfless act.

But then, in the middle of the cheering, there's a collective gasp. Is that? No, it couldn't be...but it is! None other than *Betty Fucking Jesus* emerges from Mordor's flames—her hair in place, her smile intact, and confidently doing The Classic Movie Slow Stride of Victory.

Straight to her birthday party.

Oh hell yeah. That shit gets the blood pumping. *That's* the kind of thing I want to be a part of.

Jesus, God incarnate, doesn't send down lightning bolts from the sky. He doesn't make a deal to balance the scales of divine justice or satiate any kind of divine wrath by offering himself in our place.

No, over and over again Jesus demonstrates that he's in the business of making all things new. The wrath of God? In Jesus we see that God's wrath isn't against the people God created and loves so much. God's wrath is against the hold sin and death have had over us.

And I am all about that.

In the cross and the empty tomb, God grabs Sin and Death by the throat, tells them, "you're coming with me, you sons of bitches," plunges with them into the abyss, then re-emerges victorious.

It is canon.

A WELL BEING

How dare we brand her a slut,
this woman still mourning
five husbands.
Five deaths?
Five divorces?
Deaths she couldn't prevent or
divorces she couldn't initiate,
the loss of each husband
bringing the loss of livelihood
and the chance of destitution
in a man's world.

Until finally
a sixth man takes her in.

From his house
she daily walks to the well
but she's no whore
no scarlet letter branding her
as damaged goods
no whispers around town
nor judgmental looks
with pointed fingers

The penalty for a woman
caught in adultery?
Death.
Thrown stones
bruising, breaking her body
and this woman was very much alive
drawing water to live
listening to the story of living water
from the man who knew of her life
knew of her husbands
knew of her grief
her loss
her struggle
her faith.

How dare we try
to cheapen her relational life
with a transactional accusation?

MAGNIFY

is my prolonged grief an inconvenience
to your God with a plan
a reason for everything
unquestionable omniscience?

I won't apologize for your discomfort
when I call him what he is
a heavenly sadist burning backyard bugs
with a divine magnifying glass
while the ants scurry
and search for meaning

MARY'S STORY

This was no silent night.

Cries of pain every ten, nine, eight minutes pierced the darkness, punctuated by staccato, shallow rhythmic breaths. The wise midwives back home told birthing mothers these would help get them through each contraction with at least a little less pain.

But here in this dank cave, there was no midwife. Only the smell of sheep, shit, and the sweat of Mary's labor.

There were no towels.
There was no basin of warm water.
There were no whispers of support from other women—her mother's friends, women in her family—who instinctively knew when to massage her back and shoulders, when she needed support under her arms as she knelt and cried out, and when she just needed to be. They had been there themselves. They had seen dozens of non-silent nights like these.

But none of their comfort, none of their experience—none of it was there for her.

Her husband...good Lord, he wasn't even her husband yet, was he? Oh how she loved him, but at that moment she would have traded him in a second for one of the women from Nazareth. There he stood, a nervous, immovable olive tree, not knowing the first thing about how to be helpful.

Shit. What was she going to do? She was all of thirteen, barely even able to get pregnant. Her periods had only started a bit more than a year ago, mere months before the angel's appearance. She vividly remembered the the angel's message to her, and her reaction: disbelief followed by questioning, and finally steely determination. "Here am I, the servant of the Lord; let it be with me according to your word," she had said.

And she had meant it. Every bit of it.

That last thought snapped her back into the present. "Joseph!"

He jumped a little, as the authority in her voice was nothing he had ever heard from her before.

"Joseph, come here! Now!"

Obediently, Joseph made his way to his miraculous fiancée. As he drew near, he could see the resolve in her eyes and the corners of her mouth. "Your tunic. Tear it into strips." Joseph began to protest, but Mary interrupted, calmly and firmly telling him, "The baby will need to be wiped clean. So will I. And the baby will need something to wear. Please start. Now. Over there." She pointed toward the other side of the stable. Joseph looked in the direction she was pointing and hesitated. "You can't be here when it happens. I don't think it's allowed," Mary told him. "It's okay. I'm going to be just fine."

As Joseph obediently made his way across the stable, another contraction began. Grimacing, Mary tried again to breathe as she had seen from other women. "Stay strong, stay strong, stay strong," she heard herself saying. To whom was this encouragement directed? Was it to herself? To Joseph? To the baby?

As the contraction subsided, Mary couldn't help but smile. This poor man she loved so much—ever since the angel, he had just rolled with punch after punch. What other man would believe what she had asked him to believe? There had been plenty of questions and just as many tears from both of them, but ultimately, he had trusted her. And then when she began showing, he sent her to her cousin's house so she wouldn't have to face the judging stares, the possible accusations, or even the threat of stoning. He was such a good man.

Of course, her pregnancy hadn't been the only issue. There had also been the problem of Bethlehem itself. It was relatively small, which normally she would have been thankful for. But it was also the hometown of King David, the greatest king in Israel's history. Of course, everyone wanted to claim that they had at least a little Davidic blood in them. She had known right away that Bethlehem was going to be absolutely packed. Of course, because she could pretty much go into labor at any time, their travel preparations had taken longer than normal. As a result, they hadn't begun their journey as early as they had wanted. On top of that, again because of her pregnancy, the journey itself had taken so much longer. She had walked *eighty fucking miles* with swollen ankles and a horribly aching back, all while her uterus was home to a seven-pound bundle of joy which seemed to know exactly where her bladder was and constantly tried to kick it.

When they had finally arrived, everywhere they could have possibly stayed was full. She was exhausted and just completely done, so when Joseph had come back from asking around and gingerly told her all he had been able to find was a room where animals were kept, she wasn't even upset. She could tell the time was close, and to have a covered, private place was more important than how comfortable it may or may not have been.

Yes, Joseph was a good man, and she could already tell he was the type who would do everything in his power to care for his family. She was one of the lucky ones, because it didn't always work out that way. Not with arranged marriages.

Here in Bethlehem, however, Mary could tell that he felt frustrated and incredibly guilty. He blamed himself for his lineage and the fact that they had even had to travel to Bethlehem in the first place. He blamed himself for not having all of their belongings ready quickly enough to get a head start traveling. He blamed himself for forcing her to walk because he didn't own an animal to ride on and didn't have the time or means to purchase one at the last minute. Even in their relatively short time together, Mary had gotten to know very well how his mind operated, and she could tell how relieved he felt to finally be doing something proactive and useful— even if it was as simple as tearing strips of cloth.

Her thoughts were interrupted by another contraction, and she silently cursed for getting caught up in her head instead of paying attention to how long it had been since the last one. "Three minutes," Joseph called over to her as she groaned with the sheer force of her body's determination to produce life.

"Be strong, be strong, be strong," she thought to herself again. Mary had felt so strong visiting her cousin, comparing pregnancy stories, each realizing that the other was carrying a child already marked by God. It was during her visit with Elizabeth that the full magnitude of what was happening had hit her. Elizabeth had called her *Theotokos*—God bearer. She, this kid from Galilee, had been given the awesome responsibility of bearing the Divine. And if that was the way God worked, she had asked Elizabeth, what else might God do? Shatter the thrones of the powerful and lift up the lowly like herself? Would God reverse the places of the rich and hungry, giving to those who were without, and casting away those who hoarded what they had? God had chosen her, a God who made the last first and the first last, an empowering God, a God who was ready to use ordinary people like her to flip the tables of power. To Mary's delight, rather than reacting with bewilderment, Elizabeth had joined right in with her younger cousin. "We are on the verge of something big," Elizabeth had told her. And Mary had answered with the same indomitability she was currently summoning in the stable. "For once, no scribe, rabbi, or even the fucking high priest himself will be able to hide or explain away that it's a woman making the miracle happen."

"Making the miracle happen," Mary murmured to herself, realizing that the latest contraction had ended. "Making the miracle happen."

Suddenly, another contraction began and she had the overwhelming urge to push. For a moment, her uncertainty returned—was she ready for this? Would she be able to bring a life into the world so far away from home, surrounded by animals, without the comfort of wise women surrounding her, and without the guiding hand or calm voice of a midwife?

She desperately tried to remember the advice she had heard at other births. Some women tried to push too early and the midwife would tell them to wait, no matter what their body was trying to do—the fullness of time had not yet come. But how did they know? As both the pain and the urge to push continued to grow, Mary realized something. "God," she exclaimed, "you are my midwife."

This was no imperative. It was a realization.

Strengthened, she leaned her back against the wall with her feet against the floor, legs spread and knees up. Reaching forward, Mary felt between her legs. Her cervix was dilated to the point where...was that her baby's head? No, it couldn't be. Not yet.

She felt again. Yes, there it was! What had the midwives called it back home? Crowning?

Almost on cue, the next contraction began. "My child," the Divine Midwife whispered in her ear. "You are not alone. A great cloud of witnesses surrounds you, women from every time and place. They will be holding you up, my child, as you do this miraculous thing."

"Now push."

Mary instinctively grabbed her legs below the knees, drawing them to her chest. As her pain grew stronger, she pushed with all the strength she could muster. An almost indescribable, primal sound arose from deep within her as she strained.

Mary knew that sound—she had heard it from other women, who had heard it from others, all the way back to Eve. She could feel them surrounding her—all her forebears in motherhood—just as the Divine Midwife had promised. Their strength became her strength as she pushed with all her might, beads of sweat forming on her forehead as she cried out from the pain and the pressure.

Suddenly, the pressure subsided as her baby boy's head emerged. Letting go of her legs, she reached down, cradling his head in her hands while the contraction slowly subsided.

"Very good, my child," intoned The Midwife. "What happens next will happen quickly. You will feel your son's body turn. Do not pull on him, just let your body make the miracle happen."

"Make the miracle happen," Mary repeated.

"After he turns, one long last push will bring him into the world," The Midwife continued. "Now, be ready."

The contraction began. "Little pushes for now, my blessed child. Not too much. Just let his shoulders turn. Breathe, breathe…"

Suddenly, the company of sainted women surrounding Mary were breathing in time with her, inhaling traces of Eden, exhaling the breaths of women like Tamar, Hagar, Rachel, Dinah, and the countless others whose voices had been lost to the centuries.

Her hands still cradling the baby's head, Mary did as the Divine Midwife had told her. She soon felt the baby's shoulders turning.

"Okay, my child. One last, long push."

Mary screamed as she pushed with every ounce of energy she had. She could feel the baby's body move a little, but not nearly enough.

"Keep it up, child," the Divine Midwife encouraged. "The reign of God is near. The One to defeat death is about to be born, right into your blessed hands."

And with that, the baby's shoulders pushed past the cervix.

Hands between her legs, back pressed against the wall, Mary grabbed her son as he entered the world he had created.

There was no crying. Why was there no crying? Mary quickly glanced downward. There, she saw the umbilical cord wrapped around her little boy's neck like a serpent. And instead of the light brown color she had expected, his face was turning blue.

Without waiting for any direction, she lifted the baby slightly with one hand, and with the other expertly pulled the cord over her son's head. Almost immediately, the color began to return to his face, and after a long, agonizing couple of seconds, he began to cry.

It was the most beautiful sound she had ever heard.

"Well done, good and faithful servant," whispered The Midwife.

Mary glanced over at the other side of the stable. She saw the grin on Joseph's face, and in the light of the moon noticed he had tears glistening on his cheeks. But he wasn't walking over yet, despite hearing the child's cries. Mary smiled as she realized he was probably awaiting direction from her. This was the one situation where a woman had complete control, and she wasn't ready to give that up quite yet.

Reaching forward between her legs, Mary began lifting her baby so she could hold him before realizing that the cord was still attached, and that she had nothing with which to cut it.

Shit.

While she knew that some women delayed the cord cutting until the placenta naturally detached, Mary didn't have that luxury where she was. She looked around her to find something, anything, that would help.

There, illuminated by the stars outside, a stray nail lay on the floor, partially covered by hay. Grabbing it, she brought it close to her face for a better look. Mary had already spent enough time with her husband-to-be that she immediately recognized it as Roman-made. While the nail wasn't a perfect solution to her problem by any means, it looked like the best one available at the moment. "Heaven forbid anything about tonight should be normal," she sardonically chuckled.

Leaning forward, she held the cord against the floor with one hand, and with the other tried to use the edge of the sharp end as a makeshift knife. It only took a few swipes before the cord began to give way. Mary sped up her pace as blood began to seep out. Finally, she had cut all the way through. Quickly setting down the nail, she tied the end of the cord still attached to her in a small knot and took a deep breath.

She could finally hold her baby.

Mary used her robe to wipe some of the blood and vernix off the baby as he cried and squirmed. Not too much—she wanted Joseph to feel useful when he eventually came over with his rags, but enough to help her feel a little more confident that he wasn't going to slip out of her arms.

She cradled her newborn son to her chest, and slowly, his cries began to subside. Mary could feel him snuggling into the crook of her arm, and he almost immediately began rooting, his mouth blindly searching for her nipple.

She adjusted him, and holding one breast in her hand, guided his mouth. And in his very first miracle on earth, the baby almost immediately latched on.

The Divine Midwife silently looked on as this teenage girl, a child herself, fed the Almighty God with her own body.

Mary was finally about to call Joseph over to help finish cleaning the baby off and to begin wrapping him in the cloth bands when suddenly, she saw something black swishing in the straw.

She quickly realized it was a snake. As a little girl, sometimes snakes would wander in to their house, often toward the cooking area where they could find warmth. From an early age, her mother had taught her how to identify them, so she would know which snakes she could just leave alone, and which were poisonous.

This one was a dangerous viper. And it was approaching her. If it bit her, she would almost certainly die. And what then of her baby? Still sitting on the floor like this, her little boy would be in danger too.

Without another thought, Mary stood up. Her legs were still shaking from the strain of childbirth, but she didn't even notice as she watched the poisonous serpent approach. Even if God hadn't entrusted her with this divine child, even if her boy wasn't destined to grow up and change the world, she still would've burned with the same protective anger she felt in that moment. The serpent stopped right in front of her and began to raise its head to strike her ankle.

Without a sound, Mary lifted her foot and slammed her heel into the top of its head, crushing it against the floor. Putting all her weight on that heel, she swiveled her foot back and forth, feeling the inside of the viper's head cracking and snapping. With a mother's rage, she kept crushing it until the serpent's tail lay motionless.

Mary kicked the carcass away and returned to her spot against the wall. With the confidence that comes when a person knows they've just done something significant, she called, "Joseph! Come meet your son!"

He who had been so patient ran to her, robes flapping. Joseph knelt down beside Mary, eyes wet with tears. "I am so proud of you, darling," he whispered, voice quivering. "You are the bravest woman I know." Joseph paused, trying to find the right words. "And our baby...um, your baby...is so beautiful."

"*Our* baby," Mary gently corrected him. "*You* are the one who will teach him Torah. *You* are the one who will pass your trade along to him. It doesn't matter how the story began. *You* will love him as a father loves his son."

Eyes, glistening with gratitude, Joseph stroked the baby's head. Suddenly, he stopped and looked at her. "Mary, did I see you standing up earlier? What was it?"

"Oh, it was nothing," she reassured him. "My legs were cramped. I needed to stretch them. Now, bring those rags over here so you can finish cleaning your son off. And make sure you save some—I'm going to be delivering the afterbirth soon."

"The what? I thought you were all done with...this." Joseph thought for a moment. "Isn't that a job for a midwife? Do you need me to step away again until it's...done?" He fidgeted.

Mary smiled again. Poor, adorable man whom she loved so much. He was so knowledgeable about so many things, but when it came to babies and especially childbirth, he was as clueless as most men she knew. "It's okay, my love. Take your son." She handed the baby to him. Still kneeling, Joseph gingerly cradled him.

"Am I doing it right?"

"You're doing fine," Mary reassured him. "Finish wiping him off, then wrap those cloth bands around him. And find someplace to lay him. I'll stay here until I'm done." Leaning back against the wall again, she sighed and and took a moment for contemplation while she could. Looking around, she soaked in the entire scene: the animals, the hay, Joseph with the baby, the mixture of smells and sounds, their distance from home, the closeness of the women saints and the Divine Midwife, even the serpent whose head she had crushed beneath her heel.

Mary treasured all these things, and pondered them in her heart.

LAZARUS, COME OUT

When Lazarus died, Jesus cried—
no, he wept at the grave
but not because he hadn't saved
his friend at the end.
He knew, soon, with a loud shout, he'd cry
"Lazarus, come out!"
But Mary was wailing
With Martha assailing Jesus
with protestations and accusations:
did he not even care?
Why wasn't he there when his friend,
her brother, was sick unto death, then
had taken his final breath?
Jesus had known,
he should have flown to Lazarus's bedside.
But he hadn't even tried.
Thanks to Jesus, Lazarus had died.

And Jesus cried—no, he wept
as Mary lamented and Martha kept
reminding Jesus of the power
he had to heal at life's final hour
he didn't let death devour

even complete strangers,
no—death cowered in fear
before the Son of God
so why not here?

And Jesus cried—no, he wept
but told those gathered, Lazarus slept
and Mary mourned with Martha scoffing
at Jesus's mocking of their pain
by saying they would see him again
the same sick platitude they'd heard all day
from those who meant well, but couldn't they
just say something about the here and now?
"Lord, I know my Torah, but how
is his resurrection at the end of time
any correction for *this* time?
I miss my brother here, today,
and while it's great in a different way
since I say as I pray when the final day comes
the dead will be raised,
the way that it's used
just sounds like another lame bullshit excuse
(please pardon my French).
But smell the stench from his grave over there.
It isn't fair,
Jesus Christ! Where were you?"

As Mary cried and Martha asked why,
Lazarus slept, and Jesus wept

for love of them and love for those who,
he knew, would see what he was going to do
as the final straw,
a blatant disregarding of the law.
The powers that be assumed that he,
no matter the tricks up his blasphemous sleeve
was a man, not divine. Despite the signs
he performed, how could this fraud
call himself God?
A devilish danger to the faith,
a delusional carpenter with a lathe.
Telling tall tales of his glory,
false stories deserving of death,
with each self-condemning breath?

So Jesus cried—no, he wept
for his friends, who to the end, kept
getting it wrong as much as the
Sanhedrin throng and strong Roman leaders
who'd conspire, and inspired by betrayal
after supper at the table
would arrest him, try him, flog him, crucify him,
secure their hold and their control,
asserting their way
(at least for three days).

But the power of God in their very midst,
the power of life which raised Lazarus,
didn't come to an end with a betrayer's kiss
as Jesus emerged from death's dark abyss.

UNWRITTEN RULES

Even if
the driver's been stuck before or
they'll be stuck again or
their tires are treadless or
they made a stupid driving choice or
they can't afford their payments or
they have too many kids to fit in one car or
they weren't properly prepared for the weather or
they're a convicted felon or
they don't have documentation

there's an unwritten rule in the snowy places
those regions where each year for a season
frozen white crystal drifts
create fantasy wind sculptures
while snowplow music echoes across the hills:

when a car is stuck, you help push it out.

PEACE

Existing as delicate wing feathers on a newly hatched dove
still unable to fly
or leave the nest while her mother searches
far and wide for dry land after the flood
which had hit as a crashing deluge
dealing death to life
dark waves washing over
cities and monuments
capitals and stock markets
our insular comfort shattered
in a flood of our making despite
Noah's dire warnings

She returns with hope.

Existing as olive branch sustenance
strengthening the nest
with nation-healing leaves
strengthening the fledgling
so when this new strong life
takes leave of the certain,
nudged into the uncertain air
those fragile feathers will catch the breeze—

a miracle of physics propelling it
to forlorn flood-struck places

the waters drying beneath her beating wings

OF CYCLES AND CONNECTIONS

"What's the logical point of celebrating New Year's Day?" a coworker asked me yesterday. All we could come up with from a purely logical standpoint is that it gave us a chance to recover from New Year's Eve, whether it was from consuming adult beverages, eating too much, or just staying up too late.

Which, as far as logic goes, didn't give us much to work with.

I mean, celebrating New Years isn't about logic, is it? This is a celebration meant to mark nothing more than the passage of time. It's a day that reminds us of the cyclical nature of reality. Days come and go. The seasons turn, the sun's rays in turn grow longer then shorter, we experience rain and warmth and cool and frost and snow.

But it always comes around again.

When the sun goes down and night falls, we know morning will come. When spring turns to summer, then to autumn and finally winter, we know spring will again arrive and the earth will warm and become welcoming once more. And so the marking of another year, which is a linear event, actually brings us back to the many cycles we experience in and around us.

We mark the day, we celebrate the year past or wish it good riddance, we look ahead with hope to the new year before us, we make resolutions and strive to be better parents or spouses or friends or people.

Something inside of us resonates with this symbolic turning of the wheel.

"In the beginning, God created the heavens and the earth." This is where Scripture starts us out, with the creation of all things. The how or when isn't nearly as important as the who and the what. God created. God began with light. The sun and the stars, all set in their courses, beginning this heavenly, holy rhythm that resonates today deep within us.

The new year connects us to the beginning of all things.

"Behold, I am making all things new." These are the words of the risen and reigning Christ in the book of Revelation. This passage points us ahead to the New Jerusalem, to the coming of Christ, to the river of life watering the tree whose leaves are for the healing of the nations.

From all new things to all things new, God continues to create, to bring the universe full circle from that very first creation.

It's a work whose pinnacle was on the cross and the empty tomb, and which will come to its culmination when Jesus returns. And so we live in what theologians call the "now but not yet," the fancy term for which is *prolepsis.* It's a living into the future hope we find in Jesus, a hope that still experiences pain and suffering and sin today, but a hope that is confident that all things are being made new.

Doesn't that sound an awful lot like how we tend to approach
the new year?

No, there's not much that's logical about celebrating a new year. But there
IS something innately human and beautiful about doing so, something
that simultaneously connects us both to the beginning of time and the end,
something that allows us to recognize that even in the midst of whatever
crazy randomness we may be experiencing, we are connected to the very
order of creation.

The cycle of a year ends, a new one begins. The sun goes down, the sun will
rise again. And the One who created it all continues to create—in that One
we are a new creation as we join in the work of making all things new.

DOUBT

They renamed him Doubting
as if his desire
to see
    touch
    feel
    experience
    understand
was a character flaw

 I'm awaiting my long distance friend
(the chronically late one)
The once-again-not-here one.
My imagination flips with a half twist
without sticking the landing (garnering a
low score from the East German judge).
He suffers from chronic tardiness
but not three hours resembling days
in this unwanted advent waiting—
maybe this time
maybe this time
maybe this time is the time he fell asleep
a-cross the barren Iowa interstate with
no cell service for messages from the Great

Beyond.
I'm expected to just take his presence
on belief?
My wife reassures my gymnastic mind
but I still doubt
I still wonder
until I can see
        touch
        feel
        experience
        understand
like Thomas.

THE NIGHT BEFORE

Jesus sighed.

He had lain down hours ago, but still had yet to fall asleep. Eyes wide open, he stared blankly at dark nothingness, then with another sigh rolled onto his back. A thought crossed his mind, curling the edges of his mouth almost imperceptibly into an almost sardonic half-smile. "So this is what they call 'the sleep of the just,'" he thought.

He turned his head to the left–there, not too far away, he could make out Peter's silhouette. Jesus chuckled softly. Peter was easy to pick out in the crowd of sleeping disciples. Yes, he was a big, burly man—the stereotypical Galilean fisherman. But what made it even easier to identify *Petros*, even with very little light around them, was the snore. In the daytime, James and John may have been the Sons of Thunder, but Peter's snoring definitely qualified him for that distinction when it came time to sleep. Jesus made a mental note to find a good time tomorrow to tell Peter that play on words. He'd appreciate it.

But it had to be tomorrow.

That intrusive thought erased his smile, bringing him back to where he was and why he couldn't sleep in the first place. Rolling on his side once more, Jesus propped up his head with his left hand and looked around.

There, sleeping on the dirt, were James and John, Andrew, Thomas, Phillip, Judas...

Judas.

Jesus sighed heavily as he found where Judas was sleeping. Running his heart's hand over the pages of the day now ended, it was all he could do to keep from groaning out loud. The whispers had already started amongst the disciples. They had begun even before the woman had come with the perfume. Jesus smiled again as he remembered the faith of that woman, the tears, that beautifully scented perfume, her hair brushing his feet...

...and Judas's rebuke.

His words had been intended to sting, and they had hit their mark, as the woman had stood there, stunned and speechless. "What a waste! The money for that perfume could have gone to help the poor!"

Judas was right, of course, but he had said the right thing for the wrong reason. Judas knew it. The disciples knew it. Jesus knew it.

And sure enough, the whispers had begun. Judas was the keeper of what little money the disciples had, and for some time a few of the others had suspected Judas of skimming his own personal "tithe" for himself.

Yes, Jesus thought, the other disciples were right to distrust Judas, but not for the reasons they imagined.

Jesus sighed yet again. Judas wasn't stealing from the communal purse. In fact, Jesus had noticed that the sound of jangling silver had grown a bit louder over the last couple of days. There hadn't been much in there when they had originally arrived in Jerusalem. In fact, he had privately been wondering how they were going to be able to afford the supplies to celebrate the Passover. But not long after the cries of "Hosanna!" had died away, the purse had suddenly become a bit fuller.

Thirty pieces of silver would be more than enough to take care of things.

Jesus knew that the Jewish authorities were looking for a way to have him killed, and as such he'd have to find a way to celebrate the Passover with his disciples in secret. It was of utmost importance that he wasn't found before the Passover. So much was riding on that detail.

So why had he sent Judas out to make the initial preparations?

Oh, Judas! Common sense dictated that anyone but Judas should be in charge of arranging a safe place for them to meet, but Jesus knew it was right. Judas was good with logistics, with detail—that's how he had ended up in charge of the communal purse in the first place. Who else in the group would have come up with the elaborate but sensible plan Judas had concocted? The next day, they would be led to a safe house by a man carrying a jug of water. Why the jug? He would almost certainly be the only man doing so, as carrying the water was normally woman's work. Once there, Judas would give a code sentence to the owner, who would lead them to an upstairs room where everything would be set up in advance for the Passover feast.

Jesus smiled. Judas could have had a career as a Roman spy, and he had told Judas as much when Judas had explained all the preparations to him earlier that day.

But Judas hadn't smiled back when Jesus had said that, nor had he been able to make eye contact. He had just mumbled a quick "thank you," uncomfortably shifting his feet.

The other disciples had no idea of the errand Jesus had sent Judas on that afternoon. The next day, Peter and John would be amazed when Jesus would have them go and find the man with the jug of water, and the safe house, and the furnished room. But such things do not just happen on their own. There must be preparation. And there's always a cost.

Always a price to be paid.

Jesus let his eyes wander again, finding each of his sleeping disciples one by one. He momentarily held his breath, listening. There was no sign of restlessness in any of them, no squirming in their sleep, no movement at all, and no sound save that of heavy sleep breathing and Peter's snoring. He stood up, carefully making his way over to where Judas lay. Gazing down, he watched Judas sleep. In the moonlight, he saw Judas' eyelids twitch. "He must be dreaming," Jesus thought. Then he knelt.

And prayed.

It was a short prayer, but one that came from the very depths of his being: "Father, forgive him, for he knows not what he does."

He knows not what he does. How could he? How could he have even the slightest inkling that with his precious thirty pieces of silver he had begun a chain of events that would change the world? How could he know that with the money he had received for Jesus' blood, he had that very day purchased the wine of Jesus's blood and the bread of Jesus's body? That he had bought a Passover lamb with the silver he had received for betraying the true Passover Lamb?

How could he know that the betrayal of one man would lead to God's victory over all that held humanity captive to sin?

Jesus sighed.

He leaned over and kissed Judas on the cheek.

Then he silently stood up, returned to where he had earlier been fidgeting so restlessly, and lay back down.

Almost immediately, Jesus fell asleep.

MAYBE IT'S A METAPHOR

You know, it could last forever and ever Amen.
Maybe this time there's not a walk-off homer
to end it all in the bottom of the ninth.
Or the sixteenth.
Or the fortieth.
Maybe this time both pitchers
throw a perfect game
and nobody goes home until imperfect happens
to break the stalemate.
Maybe this time each side
perfectly balances the score.
One for one, two for two, inning after inning
lasting until global warming or AR-15s
or removing the tags from all the pillows
finally finishes off humanity.
The lines called foul
actually mark fair territory
two rays at a perfect ninety degree angle
stretch into infinity
with the end points meeting
at the end goal of each player—

home.

BLESSING

May God bring you peace

an uncomfortable peace that stirs your soul
and beckons you outward

an albatross peace around your neck
freeing you by refusing to let you free

a loving peace dragging you toward those
you don't want to love

a graceful peace for those most needing grace
because they deserve it the least

a restless peace giving rest
to the heavy laden and the weak

a conflicted peace in conflict
with the world's goal to avoid conflict

the peace of the cross
willing to suffer for the sake of the other

and the empty tomb Easter peace
assuring you that despite the world's woundedness
and despite your own scars

the peace of God is with you always.

JUSTICE MATTERS

AS I LEFT THE COFFEE SHOP

a cardboard plea accosted me, scratched
in half-dried Sharpie, bent
at the corners from the clutching
grizzled fingers which grasped it
day after day

wondering what Jesus would do
when faced with cardboard and Sharpie and fingers
I remembered his words—
"the poor will always be with you."

so I kept walking.

ON A ROCKY HILLSIDE NEAR ABU DIS

A weathered shepherd squints into the midday sun
facial crevices tracing a map carved by the elements—
time's eternal cartographers.

Moisture from a late snow last week
robed the West Bank with a green
not normally worn in January
this hillside's winter couture typically taking the form
of dead, dry bones bleached by the Palestinian sun—
skeletal reminders of the cancerous takeover
creeping across the landscape
insidious in its seeming peacefulness.

"Settlements" sounds so benign,

pastoral outposts ringed with sheep,
guarded by shepherds as a flock by night.
But not the walled monolithic malignancies
guarded with conscripted uniforms
slicing his homeland's landscape into
                    occupied

chess board
squares,
knights and bishops slowly choking
the helpless king—
cutting off the green pastures
and still waters
of his forebears
while he and his people
exist as penned-in sheep pawns
awaiting the inevitable checkmate.

Gazing at his grazing flock,
he envies their ignorance.

MENACE

When I visited my doctor for an annual checkup
he began by examining my arm which I found strange but
found even stranger when he broke it.
I cried out in pain and surprise
(I mean, wouldn't you?) and he explained
that I was making too much of a fuss
so could I hold it down a bit, he asked
my yelling would bother others in other rooms
people who weren't making a scene
so could I be like them
and show some decency, he asked
as he twisted my arm
while the bone continued to crack.

So I tried to channel the pain
into a silent grimace because I didn't want
to be impolite
though when bone shards began to tear my flesh
I asked him kindly if he would stop because it hurt
and I was pretty sure he was making it worse
but he interrupted my protest
to gently explain that his own arm felt fine
so why should mine hurt so much

I'm afraid I began to lose my temper then
because he wouldn't stop fiddling with my arm
and I yelled and might have used some coarse language
but he kept injuring my arm
so I pulled away and as he reached for it again
I took a swing at him which I really didn't want to do.

He told me he was calling the police because his nose
was bleeding

I ran into the lobby shouting toward the nice decent people who quietly sat
And I waved my arm at them
so they would see what my doctor had done
but they shushed me
or pretended not to see
                    or hear
and one man said that the doctor
had always treated him well so why
was I making such a fuss and it was all very disturbing
which is when the police arrived
but when I ran toward them to show them what had been done to me

they riddled my body with bullets
because I was a menace

ARBERY

Oh thank god
this time exclaimed not
as a throwaway interjection
but sighed as a relieved prayer
in the general direction of the God
toward whom I often direct
such prayers

Out of the land which had birthed
a martyred King
from the stump of Ahmaud
arises a shoot of hope
a murdered martyr
still speaking justice
through twelve mouths

Not victory
but hope
Not equity
but hope

As for now
a lack of injustice looks like justice

as for now
the work continues
as for now
relief for a fleeting moment
Oh thank God

WALKIN' WILLIE NIGHT

ding dong the demon is dead
American justice once more extracting
her pound of burnt flesh as payment
to the delight of the gathered mob

their cacophonous jeer drowning out
the
still
small
voice
asking
      who would Jesus execute?

DISGUISED IN PLAIN SIGHT

I am a monster.
At least I look like one
To those who for safety's sake search
Not under the bed
But in it instead
Not behind the closet door
But on the party floor
and dance clubs
where they don't dare
lose sight of their drink
and they don't dare
have too many
and they don't dare
venture alone into the darkness
to tempt fate with a short skirt and crop top—
not when the first question would be
why she ventured alone in the darkness
wearing what she wore.
Monsters will be monsters, after all.

Monsters can hide
disguised in decency
invisibly in plain sight

No claws, no fangs, no big bad wolf in grandma's nightie
To reveal their ravenous intentions.

The prey speak up with audacity
crying out
supporting survivors
lighting candles
singing in the darkness
against the darkness
against the monsters
and it is well and good.

Expressing rage is well and good.
Taking back power is well and good.
Confronting fear
insisting "no more"
while demanding "know more"
refusing to go quietly into that dark night
it is all well and good.

But
what of us?

We who bear the mark of the toxic monster
we who have created the monsters
we who have fed the monsters
we who have become the monsters,
should not the battle be ours?
Our burden to bear?

Our moment to say "no more?"

While heroic resistance comes from without
real revolution begins from within.

WALLS

It's that time again, when
the birds return—
waves of screeching grackles
and silent sparrows flitting and flipping
like aerial figure skaters.

Our robin is back. The one who
insists on constructing a nest
on the porch light just to the left of the front door.
Most years I catch him mid-construction
and tear the whole thing down.
The next week I catch him again
and again the following week
and yet again a few days after that
(he's a stubborn little bastard).

But it's the door to our home.
I'm thinking of putting a little wall up
around the top of the light
to discourage him from returning.

I wonder if he'll stay where he belongs.

DEAD NAMES

When the invasion began
reporters broadcast updates
live from Kiev

until the Ukrainians corrected us

the name on our maps
the name we had always known

wasn't the capital's true identity
it spoke the language of oppression
it was dead to them

now the reporters
broadcast updates
live from Kyiv

I knew a man who corrected his family

the name on his birth certificate
the name they had always known

wasn't her true identity

it spoke the language of repression
it was dead to her

now this woman
wishes her family gave her
the same basic courtesy

as a place on the map

CALLING THE CHURCH TO REPENTANCE

SCARS

A scarred spirit considers the church on the corner
the familiar steeple cross casting distorted shadows
in the late morning sun

saved souls stream through the
cavernous maw of a doorway
khakis and polos, dresses and pantsuits
washed clean and made new
praying to the god who blessed their flock
and must be protected at any cost—

even the cost of a scarred spirit they had
beaten and left alongside the road
stoned to death in the town square
labeled as untouchable and cast out
condemned to the very pit of hell
with all their heart and all their soul and all their mind and all their strength
(the love of Jesus always in their hearts)

A scarred spirit walks away
finally free of the church and the steeple
and all the little people
finally free of toxic teaching and preaching

finally free from hearts so filled
with the love of Jesus
that they had scarred not only the spirit

but also the hands
and the feet.

JESUS AND THE DONALD

Author's Note: I originally wrote this piece in February, 2016. The Iowa caucus, where Donald Trump had come out of nowhere to place second among a field of 15-ish Republican candidates, had just occurred about 3 weeks earlier. Since then, Trump had come in first in New Hampshire, South Carolina, and Nevada. When putting the book together, I debated whether or not I should use this piece at all, and if I did, if it should serve simply as a jumping-off point for something new (since if anything, I feel even worse about the state of things now). Ultimately, I decided to use it, keeping it essentially as it had originally been written. I hope it's an interesting "point in time" perspective which also shows one way faith and politics can be in conversation with each other.

Ever heard of the *Pax Romana?*

It was, literally, "The Roman Peace." One goal of the ancient Roman Empire was for peace to come to the known world through the empire's conquering power. As Rome sent its armies further and further out, occupying wide swaths of Europe, Asia, and Northern Africa in the process, it kept order and control in those areas by setting up local governments answerable to Caesar and by crushing any dissent decisively and immediately.

For a time, the empire was stable. But was the *Pax Romana* truly peace? While it was a (relative) lack of armed conflict, the Empire ruled through fear. Intimidation. Violence.

It demanded complete allegiance to Caesar, and punished any departure from that allegiance with torture and death.

Jesus was not the first person Rome hung on a cross. The cross was a very well-known weapon of intimidation throughout the Roman Empire. Dissidents and criminals were hung on crosses, and those crosses were placed along well-traveled roads or on the outskirts of towns. Travelers had the distinct pleasure of witnessing slow suffering, often over a matter of days.

The cross was Rome's clear message to the people: Think you're gonna fuck with us? Here's what will happen.

Why am I so upset about Donald Trump's recent rise to become the GOP presidential front runner? A large reason is that his rhetoric is so reminiscent of the promise of the *Pax Romana*. He has tapped into a vein of fear and uncertainty with which our country is currently grappling, and he has exploited it to his advantage.

The United States has changed, that's for sure. Our racial makeup as a nation has shifted dramatically. The world is less defined than it once was. The boxes and categories into which we would neatly place things have blurred. Our religious backgrounds show much more of a plurality, with a much larger percentage of our population identifying with no faith at all. Our understanding of gender, of orientation, of marriage, of societal roles—they've all seen changes. Threats are much less easily identified, and that can be disconcerting because we just don't know who we need to protect ourselves from.

I could go on and on.

For those who embraced the modern world, the rise of post-modernism has been chaotic and scary. What some of us have seen as progress, they've experienced as a giant step backward, and they long for a return to the "good old days."

So along comes a man like Donald Trump—one whose answer to the fears we experience in a world where the walls between us are crumbling is to rebuild those walls. Redefine the world as a dualism of black and white, good and evil, us and them, insiders and outsiders. Then at least we know who it is we need to fear as our enemy. We can protect ourselves and be ready to fight. We can "Make America Great Again" and bring peace for ourselves.

The Pax Americana.

Trump's vision for America looks an awful lot like the dominionism of Rome. And that is precisely what Jesus set himself over against. Time and again in the gospels, Jesus calls us to a way of life that stands in stark contrast to the way of Rome, the way of the world.

Trumpism says might makes right. Jesus said blessed are the meek, the peacemakers, and the poor of spirit.

Trumpism lives with a dog-eat-dog mentality. Jesus says we are to bear one another's burdens and pray for our enemies.

Trumpism says there are the deserving and there are the losers. Jesus says all are welcome.

Trumpism says we should fear the other. Jesus says welcome the stranger.

Trumpism says the one who ends up with the most toys wins. Jesus calls us to use what we have been given for the sake of others.

Trumpism says fighting back will preserve your life. Jesus says those who try to save their life will lose it, and those who lose their life for the sake of the gospel will save it.

Trumpism uses crosses of fear and guilt and destruction and bullying and intimidation to gets its way. Jesus IS The Way, and that way is the way of the cross, the way that empties itself and dies in order that new life may spring forth through God's power of resurrection.

There is nothing of Christ in Donald Trump's vision of America. The amount of support he's gotten from Americans in general is embarrassing, but even more embarrassing is the amount of support he has received from Christians and Christian groups.

Reasonable people can and do have widely varying opinions on what constitutes a Christian response to any given situation, and I have great respect for many of my Christian siblings whose approach to political solutions opposes my own. But what I see in Donald Trump goes beyond a difference of opinion or a difference in philosophy or a difference in political viewpoint. It's an entire worldview which is dangerous and runs completely counter to the good news of the gospel.

We should be ashamed of ourselves. We should know better. And we should be more than a little worried about what that says about the state of Christianity in America.

BROKEN

They called you broken
born under a curse
forsaking them and their rules
completely unable to do right
a natural screwup
that's just how broken people are

They told you this is the only way
this is your only hope
this can fix you but nothing else can
because you're broken

They told you every wrong action
has an equal and opposite reaction
as they distanced themselves ever further away
(your broken life disgusted them)
and the only way back
was to say this thing
and believe this other thing
and do this third thing
and you would still be broken
but at least accepted

So you said the thing
and you believed the other thing
And the third thing, well you did that too
and you waited for the warm embrace of acceptance
which never came because after all

you're broken
said your boyfriend
said your girlfriend
said your spouse

and it made sense
because your God had said it first

JESUS FLAG

What sort of flag would Jesus fly?
What sign of power demanding allegiance
raises proudly as we pledge fealty,
devoting ourselves to defending it?
What banner rides ahead of the Divine Army as
it gallops into holy warfare?

Would it be red like the blood shed by his enemies
or like his blood shed for his enemies?
White for doctrinal purity
or for the Bethlehem star over a humble stable?
Blue for the meting out of justice against the guilty
or for the establishment of justice for the oppressed?

Would the Jesus Flag fly above halls of power
or be hoisted in protest outside them?
Would it fly in opposition to foreign flags
or as a reminder of our unity as children of God?
Would it be raised to signal a military attack
or to signal the peace which passes all understanding?
Would it be synonymous with patriotism
or lie draped over nationalism's coffin?

What sort of flag would Jesus fly
and why does the one in the sanctuary
have stars and stripes?

FEAR, SUFFERING, AND A LITTLE GREEN DUDE

In the movie *The Phantom Menace*, Yoda says, "Fear leads to anger. Anger leads to hate. Hate leads to suffering."

The little green dude had a pretty good handle on human nature.

So much of the suffering we see in the world has fear at its root. Usually, that means fearing the loss of something like one's safety, power, money, possessions, ideas, comfort, or privilege. Part of the (*cue gratuitous Star Wars reference*) "dark side" of human nature shows itself when we allow those sorts of fears to guide our decision-making. Suddenly, we can justify just about any action against any perceived threat.

That's when the really bad shit happens.

Really bad fear-based shit is an age-old human problem, but we currently live in a time where both the fear and the shit have higher stakes and bigger consequences than perhaps at other times in history. Individuals, governments, and churches have reacted with fear to many of the changes post-modernity has brought with it. Fear multiplies fear, so to protect ourselves, we have built fortresses of safety and have armed ourselves either with actual weapons or with the weapons of words, intimidation, and policy.

It all reminds me so much of the events after Jesus's birth (at least in Matthew's gospel). When Jesus is born, King Herod's reaction to the news is the same fear-based shit we see every day in the headlines. Herod was narcissistic, a liar, and one who used his position to further his own interests, often to the detriment of his subjects (good thing we haven't dealt with anyone like *that* lately in American politics, right?). He was also paranoid and ruthless—a deadly combination. Herod was literally the King of the Jews, allowed to rule as long as he played nicely with the occupying Roman forces.

But he himself wasn't a Jew.

Understandably, Herod had just a bit of imposter syndrome. And he was constantly afraid that his power might be taken away, or that someone might think he was an illegitimate ruler and kill him. The man saw conspiracies everywhere. He even had two of his sons and one of his wives executed for treason.

So when a bunch of foreign astrologers (those are the wise men, or magi) show up and tell him the King of the Jews had just been born, that scares the shit out of him. I love how he quickly gets himself together and tries to play it off. "Um...so when you find the kid, let me know, okay? I would like to 'worship' him as well." (This is the moment where in a movie version, he would give a side eye smirk to the camera, and we would know Jesus was in very real danger.)

But then the magi go and do something completely unexpected—they *don't* return to Herod with Jesus's temporary Bethlehem address plugged into Google Maps. Instead, they head straight home. They even take a different route, just to be safe.

When Herod gets wind of what had happened, he pretty much goes ballistic. He was not about to stand idly by while some Jewish baby grew up and prepared to steal his throne. So he did a little math, coming to the conclusion that if his soldiers murdered every kid in the Bethlehem metro area aged two years or younger, he should be safe.

So that's exactly what he ordered.

Suddenly, the Christmas story is no longer about romanticized celebrations with animals and child shepherds in bathrobes and "little Lord Jesus, no crying he makes." Instead, we're forced to grapple with a hard reality: when we make political, personal, or religious decisions based in fear, when our primary goal becomes not losing what we feel ought to be ours, the result is violence and oppression.

Fear leads to anger. Anger leads to hate. Hate leads to suffering.

We as individuals have become Herod.

We as a nation have become Herod.

We as a church have become Herod.

People, we've got to repent. Too many kids from Bethlehem have already died. We've got to quit letting fear dictate our decision-making. Especially those of us who are Christian—is it really a mark of faith when we're living as though we don't already know the end of the story?

(*Spoiler alert: love wins.*)

HYMN POEMS

IN HOPEFUL EXPECTATION

Tune: *Herzlich Tut Mich Verlangen*
(O Sacred Head Now Wounded)

As we await fulfillment
Of God's long-promised reign
The coming of a savior
To set things right again
Lord bring your righteous mercy
To all who gather here
In hopeful expectation
Of Jesus coming near

Injustice rules the nations
And people flee in fear
To refuge in a new land
But they're not welcomed here
Fill hearts with your compassion
To us your Spirit send
In hopeful expectation
Of love that has no end

Your advent, Lord, we pray for
Come quickly, Prince of Peace!

Incarnate God, be near us
And make all suffering cease
But as we wait empower us
To do your work on earth
In hopeful expectation
Of our messiah's birth

MUSTARD SEED FAITH

Tune: SLANE (Be Thou My Vision)

Sometimes we wonder if faith is in vain
Where is your kingdom, God? Where is your reign?
Questioning ourselves, we ask, "Lord, how long?"
Why must lament be our cry and our song?

Jesus says faith can be small like a seed
But it can do more than we'll ever see.
Even when our souls feel by doubt they are plagued,
Faith can move mountains, changing night into day.

Faith is a gift from God, not human made,
Jesus can form it, transform it each day.
Though it doesn't feel like enough, it will be—
Faith that moves mountains from a small mustard seed.

Mary in the garden that first Easter morn
Jesus appeared to her, faith was reborn.
She was the first apostle, God gave all she'd need:
Faith that changed all the world from a small mustard seed.